The Wish

Contents

The Wish	4
A Night at the Fair	12
Lucky	21
Vocabulary	30
Story Questions	32

Titles in the Runway series

Level 4
The Street
The Wish
The Magic Shop
The Ghost House

Level 5
Trapped
The Rumour
The Food Museum
Escape from the City

Level 6
The Good Student
Virtual Teacher
Football Smash
The Empty House

Badger Publishing Limited
Oldmedow Road,
Hardwick Industrial Estate,
King's Lynn PE30 4JJ
Telephone: 01438 791037
www.badgerlearning.co.uk

4 6 8 10 9 7 5

The Wish ISBN 978 1 84691 366 2

Text © Alison Hawes, Keith West, Jillian Powell 2008
Complete work © Badger Publishing Limited 2008
Second edition © 2014

All rights reserved. No part of this publication may be reproduced, stored in any form or by any means mechanical, electronic, recording or otherwise without the prior permission of the publisher.

The right of Alison Hawes, Keith West and Jillian Powell to be identified as the authors of this Work has been asserted by them in accordance with the Copyright, Designs and Patents Act 1988.

Publisher: David Jamieson
Commissioning Editor: Carrie Lewis
Design: Fiona Grant
Illustration: Seb Camagajevac, Enso Troiano, Paul Savage

The Wish

Written by Alison Hawes
Illustrated by Seb Camagajevac

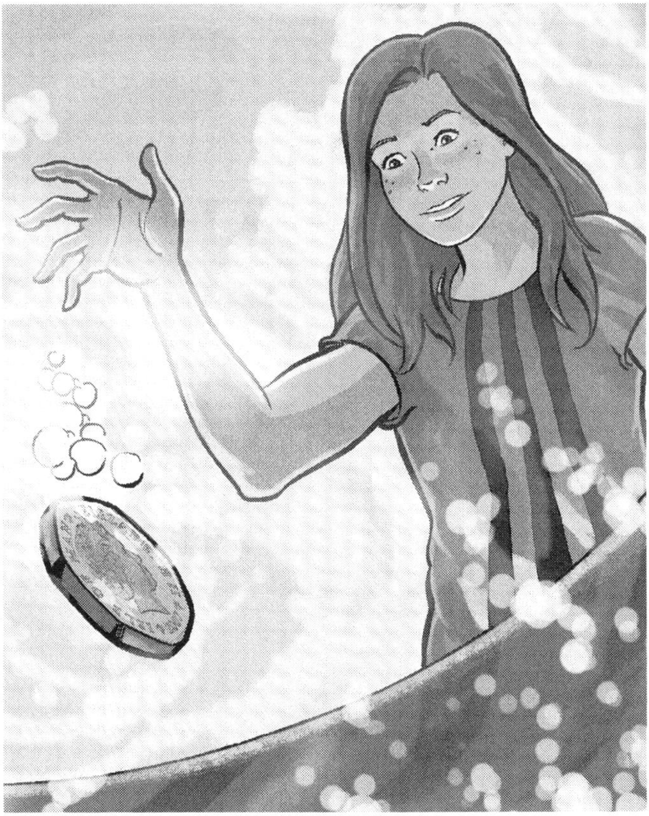

On Sunday, Jane made a wish.
She wished she was a celebrity.

On Monday, Jane was in the papers!

On Tuesday, Jane was on T.V!

On Wednesday, Jane went to the shops.
Lots of people wanted her autograph!

On Thursday, Jane went swimming.
Lots of people wanted her photo!

On Friday, Jane met her brother.

On Saturday, Jane was in the papers again!

Jane wanted to see her friends.
But lots of people wanted to see Jane!

On Sunday, Jane stayed at home.

That day, Jane wished she wasn't a celebrity.

But it was too late!

A Night at the Fair

Written by Keith West
Illustrated by Enzo Troiano

It was the night of the fair.
Adam and Clare had five pounds.

Adam went on the dodgems.
He had three rides.

Clare went on the pirate ship.
She had two rides.

Adam went on the coconut shy.
He won four prizes!

Adam and Clare went on the rollercoaster.
They had one ride!

Clare smiled.

She took out her phone and went to the rollercoaster.

"Smile!"

Lucky

Written by Jillian Powell
Illustrated by Paul Savage

Six friends played the lottery.
They each chose a number.

The first chose his house number.

The second chose his birthday.
The third chose her mum's birthday.

The fourth chose the number of his favourite football player.

The fifth chose his daughter's birthday.

The last chose his son's age - 17.

On Saturday the lottery was on TV.

2   7   8   10   15   17

They had won!

But one man knew they had not won.

That day was his son's 18th birthday.
He had chosen the number 18.

Vocabulary

The Wish

Sunday
Monday
Tuesday
Wednesday
Thursday
Friday
Saturday
wish
celebrity
people
autograph
swimming

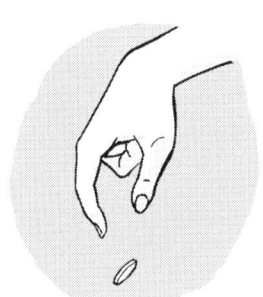

A Night at the Fair

one
two
three
four
five
fifty
fair
pounds
money
dodgems

rides
pirate ship
coconut shy
prizes
rollercoaster
hungry

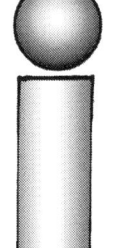

Lucky

first
second
third
fourth
fifth
sixth
number
March
July

played
lottery
house
birthday
chose
favourite
daughter
son
age
won

Story questions

The Wish

When was Jane on TV?
Who did Jane meet on Friday?
Does Jane like being a celebrity?

A Night at the Fair

Who went on the pirate ship?
How many prizes did Adam win?
How did Clare get more money?

Lucky

What number did the third friend choose?
Who chose 15?
Why didn't the friends win?